VERONICA RUFF

A Gentle Mother's Day Devotional

For Mothers, Those Who Miss Them, and Those Who Long to Be

*For every mother,
for those who miss their mothers,
and for those who long to be—
with love.*

"She is clothed with strength and dignity;
she can laugh at the days to come."
— Proverbs 31:25 (NIV)

Contents

Introduction   1

Day 1   3

Day 2   5

Day 3   7

Day 4   9

Day 5   11

Day 6   13

Day 7   15

Lessons from Mary   17

Lesson 1   18

Lesson 2   20

Mary at the Cross   22

A Blessing for You   24

Journal Page   25

Journal Page   26

Journal Page   27

Journal Page   28

Journal Page   29

Journal Page   30

Journal Page   31

About the Author   32

Also by Veronica Ruff   33

Introduction

Mother's Day can be a beautiful day.

It can also be a tender one.

For some, it is filled with laughter, hugs, and the quiet joy of being surrounded by children and family.

For others, it carries an ache—of loss, of longing, of memories that feel both close and far away.

This devotional has been created gently, with all of these hearts in mind.

It is for the mother who is pouring out love each day, often unseen.

For the woman who misses her mother deeply.

For the one who longs to become a mother.

For those who mother in ways that may never be recognised, but are deeply meaningful.

You are not forgotten here.

Over the next seven days, you are invited to pause.

To breathe.

To sit quietly with God, even if only for a few moments.

Each day offers a short Scripture, a gentle reflection, a prayer, and a space to consider what God may be speaking to your heart.

There is no pressure to do this perfectly.

No expectation to feel a certain way.

Simply come as you are.

You may choose to read one day at a time leading up to Mother's Day, or slowly return to these pages whenever your heart needs rest.

At the end of this devotional, you will also find a small collection of reflections on Mary—a mother who walked a path of deep trust, quiet strength, and profound love.

May you find comfort here.

May you feel seen.

And may you be reminded that you are deeply loved.

Day 1

A Mother's Love Reflects God

"She is clothed with strength and dignity;
    she can laugh at the days to come.
    She speaks with wisdom,
    and faithful instruction is on her tongue."
    — Proverbs 31:25–26 (NIV)

There is something deeply powerful about a mother's love.
    It is often found in the quiet, unseen moments—
    in the meals prepared, the comforting words spoken, the countless small
acts of care that may go unnoticed by the world, but are never unseen by God.
    Motherhood is not always loud or celebrated.
    More often, it is steady. Faithful. Given freely, day after day.
    And in these ordinary moments, something extraordinary is happening.
    A mother's love reflects the heart of God.
    In the patience you offer, even when you are tired…
    In the kindness you extend, even when it is not returned…
    In the strength you carry, even when you feel weak…
    God's love is being quietly revealed through you.
    You may not always feel strong or dignified.
    You may question whether what you are doing truly matters.
    But God sees every act of love.
    Every sacrifice.

Every moment of faithfulness.

Nothing is wasted.

Whether you are raising children, remembering them, longing for them, or nurturing others in ways that may not be recognised—your love has value. Deep, eternal value.

Today, be gently reminded:

You are reflecting something sacred.

Prayer

Lord,

Thank You for the gift of love—the kind that gives, nurtures, and endures.

When I feel unseen or unsure, remind me that You see every small act of care.

Strengthen me in the quiet moments, and help me to reflect Your love in all that I do.

Amen.

Journal Prompt

Where in your life are you quietly giving love that may go unnoticed, and how might God be working through those moments?

Day 2

Seen in the Small Things

"Whatever you do, work at it with all your heart, as working for the Lord, not for human masters."
— Colossians 3:23 (NIV)

So much of what love looks like in daily life is small.

It is found in the routines that repeat themselves day after day—

the washing, the tidying, the preparing, the checking in, the remembering of little details that matter to someone else.

These moments can feel ordinary.

Sometimes even invisible.

It is easy to wonder if they truly matter.

But God sees differently.

What feels small to us is never small to Him.

Every act of care, every quiet responsibility, every unseen effort is noticed. Not only noticed, but valued. When done with love, even the simplest task carries deep meaning.

There is no such thing as insignificant work when it is offered with a willing heart.

Whether you are caring for others, managing a home, supporting loved ones, or simply getting through the day as best you can—your efforts are not overlooked.

God is present in the small things.

And He delights in the love woven through them.

Today, instead of measuring the value of your day by what was seen or recognised, gently remember:

Nothing done in love is ever wasted.

Prayer

Lord,

Help me to see value in the small things I do each day.

When I feel unnoticed or weary, remind me that You see and cherish every act of love.

Give me strength to continue, and peace in knowing that nothing is wasted in Your hands.

Amen.

Journal Prompt

What are some small, everyday things in your life that may feel unnoticed, and how might God see them differently?

Day 3

Strength for the Weary Mother

"He gives strength to the weary
    and increases the power of the weak."
    — Isaiah 40:29 (NIV)

There are days when the tiredness runs deeper than sleep can fix.
    Days when your body feels heavy, your mind feels full, and your heart feels stretched in more directions than you can manage.
    You may still keep going—because you have to.
    Because others depend on you.
    Because love continues, even when energy is low.
    But inside, you may be quietly asking:
    How much more can I give?
    God sees that weariness.
    He does not ask you to carry everything in your own strength.
    He does not expect you to be endlessly strong.
    Instead, He offers something different.
    His strength.
    Not loud or overwhelming, but steady.
    Gentle.
    Enough for this moment.
    You don't need to have everything figured out today.
    You don't need to feel strong to keep moving forward.

Even in your weakness, God is present.

Even in your exhaustion, He is near.

And somehow, in ways you may not always notice, He is sustaining you—one small step at a time.

Today, if all you can do is pause for a moment and breathe, let that be enough.

You are not carrying this alone.

Prayer

Lord,

You see my tiredness and know the weight I carry.

When I feel weak, remind me that Your strength is enough for me.

Help me to rest in You, even in the middle of my responsibilities.

Carry me gently through this day.

Amen.

Journal Prompt

Where are you feeling most weary right now, and what might it look like to let God meet you in that place?

Day 4

Letting Go and Trusting God

"Trust in the Lord with all your heart
   and lean not on your own understanding;
   in all your ways submit to Him,
   and He will make your paths straight."
   — Proverbs 3:5–6 (NIV)

There comes a time in every mothering journey when holding on begins to look different.

What once meant protecting, guiding, and closely nurturing can slowly become stepping back, releasing, and trusting God with what we can no longer control.

This is not always easy.

Letting go can feel like losing something—

the closeness, the certainty, the sense of being needed in the same way.

It can bring questions, worries, and a quiet ache that sits beneath the surface.

But letting go is not the same as letting go *alone*.

It is an invitation to trust.

To trust that the God who entrusted you with love in the first place is still present, still guiding, still working in ways you cannot see.

Whether you are releasing grown children into the world, navigating changing relationships, or simply learning to loosen your grip on things you once held tightly—God is already there.

He sees the path ahead more clearly than we ever could.

And He holds those we love even more securely than we can.

Today, you are gently invited to open your hands just a little.

Not in fear, but in trust.

Not in loss, but in faith that God's care extends far beyond your own.

Prayer

Lord,

Help me to trust You with what I cannot control.

When I feel the pull to hold on tightly, remind me that You are already holding all things in Your hands.

Give me peace in the letting go, and confidence in Your faithful care.

Amen.

Journal Prompt

Is there something—or someone—you are finding hard to release into God's care, and what might it look like to trust Him with it today?

Day 5

For the Mother Who Grieves

"The Lord is close to the brokenhearted
  and saves those who are crushed in spirit."
  — Psalm 34:18 (NIV)

Grief has a way of making days like this feel heavier.
  While others may be celebrating, your heart may be holding something tender—
  a loss that is deeply personal, quietly carried, and not always seen by those around you.
  You may be grieving a mother who is no longer here.
  A child you have lost.
  A relationship that has changed or become distant.
  Or the longing for something that has not come to be.
  Grief does not follow a timetable.
  It does not soften simply because the calendar says it should.
  And on days like this, it can feel especially present.
  But you are not alone in it.
  God is not distant from your sorrow.
  He does not turn away from your pain or expect you to hide it.
  He draws near.
  Right into the middle of your grief.
  Right into the places that feel most fragile.

There is no need to pretend here.
No need to be strong.
Your tears are seen.
Your heart is known.
And your sorrow is held with deep compassion.
Today, if all you can do is acknowledge the ache, let that be enough.
God is close to you—especially here.

Prayer
Lord,
You see my grief and know the weight it carries.
On this day, when emotions may feel close to the surface, draw near to me.
Comfort my heart and remind me that I am not alone in this pain.
Hold me gently and give me peace, even in the midst of sorrow.
Amen.

Journal Prompt
What is on your heart today that feels tender or heavy, and how might you gently bring that before God?

Day 6

The Gift of Spiritual Motherhood

"Likewise, teach the older women to be reverent in the way they live…

Then they can urge the younger women to love their husbands and children…"

— Titus 2:3–4 (NIV)

Motherhood is not defined by biology alone.

There are countless ways a woman can nurture, guide, and love—ways that may not always be recognised, but carry deep and lasting impact.

Spiritual motherhood is found in the quiet encouragement offered at the right time…

In the listening ear…

In the wisdom shared gently…

In the care extended to those who need it most.

It is seen in those who walk alongside others, offering support, kindness, and guidance without needing a title or recognition.

These expressions of love matter.

They shape lives.

They bring comfort.

They reflect the heart of God just as beautifully as any other form of motherhood.

If your path has looked different than you expected…

If you have longed for something that has not come to be…

Or if your role has taken a shape you did not anticipate—
Your capacity to nurture has not been lost.
It is simply being expressed in a different, meaningful way.
God uses every act of love.
Today, be gently reminded:
The love you give—however it is expressed—is valuable and needed.

Prayer

Lord,

Thank You for the many ways love can be given and received.

Help me to recognise the opportunities I have to encourage, support, and nurture those around me.

Remind me that my role has purpose, and that the love I give is never without meaning.

Amen.

Journal Prompt

Who in your life might benefit from your encouragement or care today, and how could you gently reach out to them?

Day 7

You Are Deeply Loved

"For I am convinced that neither death nor life, neither angels nor demons,
neither the present nor the future, nor any powers,
neither height nor depth, nor anything else in all creation,
will be able to separate us from the love of God that is in Christ Jesus our Lord."
— Romans 8:38–39 (NIV)

At the end of this journey, there is one truth to gently rest in:
You are deeply loved.
Not because of all that you do.
Not because of how well you hold everything together.
Not because of how others see you.
But simply because you are His.
In the busyness, in the quiet, in the joy, and in the sorrow—God's love remains constant.
It does not lessen when you feel tired.
It does not fade when you feel uncertain.
It does not disappear in moments of grief or longing.
It stays.
Steady.
Faithful.
Unchanging.

There may be days when you feel overlooked or unappreciated.

Days when your efforts feel small, or your heart feels heavy.

But none of those things define your worth.

You are known.

You are seen.

You are held.

And nothing—nothing at all—can separate you from the love of God.

As you move beyond these pages, carry this with you:

You are deeply loved, exactly as you are.

Prayer

Lord,

Thank You for Your constant and unchanging love.

When I forget who I am or feel uncertain of my worth, remind me that I am Yours.

Help me to rest in Your love and carry that truth with me each day.

Amen.

Journal Prompt

What would change in your heart or daily life if you truly rested in the truth that you are deeply loved by God?

Lessons from Mary

Reflections on trust, surrender, and a mother's love

Lesson 1

Mary's Yes to God

"I am the Lord's servant," Mary answered. "May your word to me be fulfilled."
— Luke 1:38 (NIV)

Mary's journey began with a yes.
Not a yes that came with full understanding.
Not a yes that guaranteed ease or certainty.
But a quiet, willing surrender to God.
She was asked to step into something unknown.
Something that would change her life completely.
And still, she said yes.
There is something deeply moving about that kind of trust.
Mary did not have all the answers.
She could not see the full path ahead.
Yet she chose to believe that God was faithful, even in uncertainty.
There are moments in life when we are invited into a similar place.
Moments when we are asked to trust without knowing how things will unfold.
When the future feels unclear, and the path feels unfamiliar.
Like Mary, we may not feel ready.
We may have questions, fears, or hesitation.
And yet, God does not ask for perfect understanding.
He simply invites us to trust Him.

Mary's yes was not about having everything figured out.

It was about placing her life in God's hands.

Today, you may not be facing something as extraordinary—but you may still be holding something unknown.

A decision.

A change.

A quiet uncertainty in your heart.

Perhaps the invitation is the same:

To trust.

To surrender.

To say yes to God, even in the not knowing.

Prayer

Lord,

Help me to trust You, even when I cannot see the full picture.

Give me a willing heart, like Mary, to say yes to Your plans for my life.

Calm my fears and strengthen my faith as I place my trust in You.

Amen.

Journal Prompt

Is there an area of your life where you feel uncertain, and what might it look like to trust God with it today?

Lesson 2

Raising a Child with a Divine Calling

"But Mary treasured up all these things and pondered them in her heart."
  — Luke 2:19 (NIV)

Mary's journey as a mother was unlike any other.

From the very beginning, she knew her child had been entrusted to her by God for a purpose far greater than her own understanding.

Yet even with that knowledge, she still had to walk the ordinary, everyday path of raising Him—

caring for Him, teaching Him, watching Him grow.

There is something deeply human in the way Scripture describes her.

She "treasured" and "pondered."

She didn't always speak.

She didn't always act.

Sometimes, she simply held things quietly in her heart.

There is wisdom in that kind of motherhood.

Not everything needs to be controlled.

Not every moment needs to be understood.

Sometimes, love looks like watching, trusting, and allowing space for God to work in ways we cannot.

As mothers—or as those who nurture others in any capacity—it can be tempting to hold tightly.

To guide every step.

To try and shape outcomes.

To protect from every possible hardship.

But Mary's example reminds us of something important:

Our role is not to control the outcome.

It is to love, to guide, and then to trust God with the rest.

Those we care for are not fully ours.

They are entrusted to us for a time.

God's hand is on their lives in ways we cannot always see or understand.

Today, you may be watching someone you love grow, change, or walk a path that feels uncertain.

Like Mary, you are invited to hold them with care—but also with open hands.

To treasure.

To ponder.

To trust.

Prayer

Lord,

Help me to trust You with the lives of those I love.

When I feel the need to control or worry, remind me that You are already at work.

Give me wisdom to nurture well, and peace to release what is beyond my control.

Amen.

Journal Prompt

Is there someone in your life you are finding hard to entrust fully to God, and what might it look like to hold them with both love and open hands?

Mary at the Cross

"Near the cross of Jesus stood his mother…"
— John 19:25 (NIV)

There are moments in life that cannot be fixed.

Moments where love remains, but the outcome cannot be changed.

Mary stood at the cross and watched her son suffer.

She could not intervene.

She could not take the pain away.

She could not change what was unfolding before her eyes.

All she could do was remain.

To stay.

To witness.

To love, even in the midst of unimaginable sorrow.

There is a quiet strength in that kind of presence.

A strength that does not try to control or rescue, but simply refuses to turn away.

Many will know something of this kind of love.

The love that sits beside hospital beds.

The love that carries grief that cannot be spoken.

The love that holds on, even when the heart is breaking.

Mary's presence at the cross reminds us that sometimes love looks like staying.

Not fixing.

Not understanding.

Just being there.

And in that place of deep sorrow, God was not absent.

Even in the suffering, He was at work.

Even in the heartbreak, something greater was unfolding—though it could not yet be seen.

If you are holding a place of pain today…

If you are standing in a moment that feels heavy or unresolved…

You are not alone there.

God meets you in that space.

Just as He was present at the cross, He is present with you now—

in your grief, in your questions, in your quiet endurance.

Today, you are gently reminded:

Even here, God is near.

Prayer

Lord,

In moments of sorrow and pain, help me to trust that You are near.

When I cannot understand what is happening, give me the strength to remain and the comfort of Your presence.

Hold me gently in the places that feel too heavy to carry alone.

Amen.

Journal Prompt

Is there a place in your life where you are being asked simply to "remain," and how might you invite God into that space today?

A Blessing for You

May you feel gently held in the love of God—
in the quiet moments, in the busy ones, and in everything in between.
May you know that your life, in all its seasons, carries deep meaning and value.
That nothing you have given in love has ever been wasted.
May you find rest when you are weary,
comfort when your heart feels tender,
and peace in the places where you are learning to trust.
May you be reminded, again and again,
that you are seen, you are known, and you are deeply loved.
And may you carry that love with you—
into your days, into your relationships,
and into every small, beautiful moment still to come.
Amen.

Journal Page

Reflections:

Journal Page

On My Heart Today:

Journal Page

A Quiet Moment with God:

Journal Page

What I Am Grateful For:

Journal Page

Prayers and Thoughts:

Journal Page

Where I Am Being Led:

Journal Page

Notes and Reflections:

About the Author

Veronica Ruff is a Christian author and publisher with a heart for creating gentle, faith-filled resources that bring comfort, reflection, and encouragement in life's more tender seasons.

Through Integrity Press Publishing, she writes devotionals and inspirational works designed to offer readers a quiet space to pause, breathe, and reconnect with God. Her writing is especially shaped by a desire to support those navigating grief, longing, and the often unseen moments of everyday life.

With a calm and compassionate voice, Veronica invites readers to come as they are—without pressure or expectation—and to find reassurance in God's presence.

A Gentle Mother's Day Devotional reflects her commitment to creating meaningful, accessible resources for mothers, those who miss them, and those who long to be.

More resources from Integrity Press Publishing coming soon.

You can connect with me on:

- https://linktr.ee/integritypresspublishing

Also by Veronica Ruff

Choosing Meaningful Funeral Readings, Prayers and Hymns: A Simplified Catholic & Christian Guide for Families Making Decisions Under Pressure

When someone you love dies, decisions must often be made quickly. In the midst of grief, families are asked to choose readings, prayers and hymns that will shape a final farewell.

Choosing Meaningful Funeral Readings, Prayers and Hymns is a clear and simplified guide for Catholic and Christian families who wish to make those decisions thoughtfully, without becoming overwhelmed.

After the Funeral

A Christian Companion Guide for the First Year of Grief offers gentle reflections for those walking through the early seasons of loss. Each chapter explores experiences that many grieving people encounter during the first year, accompanied by comforting Scripture and simple prayers.

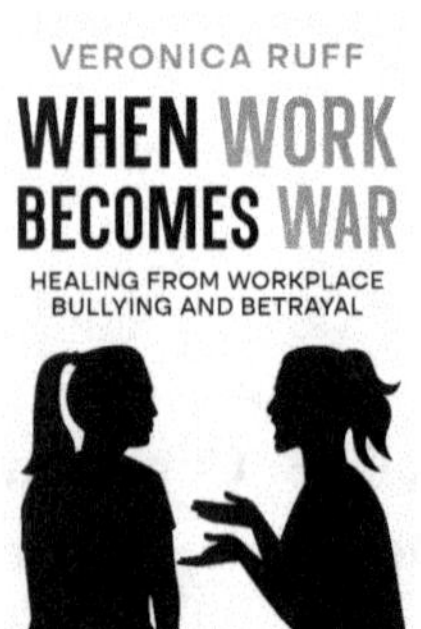

When Work Becomes War: Healing From Workplace Bullying and Betrayal

When Work Becomes War is a fierce, poetic, and unflinching testimony to the psychological toll of toxic workplaces—and to the quiet, steady power of healing and reclamation.

Drawing from lived experience, editorial clarity, and psychological insight, Veronica Ruff gives language to experiences many endure but struggle to name: gaslighting, workplace bullying, institutional betrayal, triangulation, and the systematic erosion of truth.

The Easter Colouring and Activity Book: A Gentle Collection of Easter Puzzles, Colouring Pages, and Reflections

The Easter Colouring and Activity Book is a gentle companion for children and families to enjoy together. Filled with simple devotionals, calming colouring pages, and thoughtful activities, this book invites moments of reflection, creativity, and connection throughout the Easter season.

The Easter Devotional: 40 Days of Prayer, Reflection and Family Devotions for Lent and Easter

A calm, family-centred devotional for Lent and Easter, designed to help parents and children slow down, reflect, and grow in faith together.

A Cosy Easter Table: Simple Recipes for Family, Friends, and Easy Hosting

A Cosy Easter Table is a warm and welcoming collection of simple recipes created for gathering with family and friends during the Easter season.